To

From

Date

A Special Delivery of God's
Refreshing Love

heavenly mail

words of promise from *God*

G. A. Myers

HOWARD
PUBLISHING CO.

Our purpose at Howard Publishing is to:

- *Increase faith* in the hearts of growing Christians
- *Inspire holiness* in the lives of believers
- *Instill hope* in the hearts of struggling people everywhere

Because He's coming again!

Heavenly Mail—Words of Promise from God © 2001 by Gary Myers
All rights reserved. Printed in the Mexico

Published by Howard Publishing Co., Inc.
3117 North 7th Street, West Monroe, Louisiana 71291-2227

01 02 03 04 05 06 07 08 09 10   10 9 8 7 6 5 4 3 2 1

Interior design by Steve Diggs
Edited by Philis Boultinghouse

Library of Congress Cataloging-in-Publication Data
Myers, G. A., 1955-
Heavenly mail : words of promise from God : a special delivery of God's refreshing love / G. A. Myers.
     p. cm.
ISBN 1-58229-168-3
1. Devotional literature. I. Title.
BV4812 .M93 2001
242—dc21   00-053948

Scripture quotations are from the Holy Bible, New International Version. Copyright © 1973, 1978, 1984
by International Bible Society. Used by permission of Zondervan Bible Publishers.

Delight yourself in the LORD

and he will give you the desires of your heart.

Commit your way to the LORD;

trust in him and he will do this.

Psalm 37:4–5

Contents

A Word to the Reader

Writing a letter is a special way to express yourself to someone you care for. It allows you to convey your feelings, thoughts, and emotions in a way unlike any other.

And what about receiving mail in return? Who doesn't enjoy the feeling of going to the mailbox, opening the door, and finding that you've got mail? With anticipation, you open the envelope and read the words of a cherished loved one or a faraway friend. Even though the writer is not present, you feel the warmth that the two of you share, and your hearts are united once again. That's what happens when you read *Heavenly Mail: Words of Promise from God.*

This unique book is filled with letters between someone like yourself and the very best friend of all—your heavenly Father. You'll quickly identify with the prayers, written as letters to a loving God, because they convey the needs, emotions, feelings, and struggles that life presents on a regular basis. In heaven's response, you'll read personalized, paraphrased scriptures, also written as letters, and you'll experience the assuring presence and loving warmth that only heaven can give.

The promises that fill these heavenly letters will remain with you, inspire you, and fill you with hope. Let this little book bring you closer to heaven and to the promises that will impact your todays, tomorrows, and the rest of your life.

A LETTER TO *Heaven*

Dear Father,

It's Your child again, needing You as always. I am writing about something I need help with but am ashamed to admit—especially to You, whose fearlessness is legendary and whose steps have never known retreat. I am feeling afraid. I'm not even sure what it is I'm afraid of, but it certainly is real. Maybe it's the uncertainty of the future or even my failures of the past. It could be the deeper sense of responsibility I'm feeling for friends and family. I'm apprehensive about letting down those I love most. You see, they have expectations of me that I'm not sure I can fulfill. I'm fearful I won't meet my own expectations, let alone those of others.

I've heard the stories of how You have led the charge in situations that others considered a lost cause, how You have strengthened the legs of the timid and restored honor and promise to those who have fled in fear.

I don't want to be afraid any longer. I want to live a courageous life, but I need to hear from You. Only Your words of courage and confidence will renew my strength and stiffen my resolve for today's trials and tomorrow's tests.

Your Child Who Needs Your Courage

A LETTER FROM *Heaven*

Dear Child Needing Courage,

I'm glad you came to Me about this. I want you to be strong and courageous, not afraid or terrified by anything or anyone, because I go with you wherever you go. I will never leave you or forsake you. I'll say it again: I am out in front of you, going before you. I will never leave you or fail you, so you do not have to be afraid or discouraged. You do not need to fear disgrace or be afraid of humiliation, and believe Me, you will forget the shame of your past.

I have rescued you, called your name, and made you Mine. Whether you are walking through waters or crossing rivers, you will not drown. Even when you face a firestorm, you will remain unharmed. I will make you strong and will help you through every trial. I will support and rescue you with My right hand. I will grasp your hand, so you do not need to be afraid. Remember, I did not give you a spirit of timidity, but a spirit of power, love, and self-discipline.

Your Caring Father in Heaven

from Deuteronomy 31:6, 8
Isaiah 54:4; 43:1–3; 41:10–13; 2 Timothy 1:7

God's Word OF PROMISE

ISAIAH 43:1–3

Fear not, for I have redeemed you; I have summoned you by name; you are mine. When you pass through the waters, I will be with you; and when you pass through the rivers, they will not sweep over you. When you walk through the fire, you will not be burned; the flames will not set you ablaze. For I am the LORD, your God, the Holy One of Israel, your Savior.

PSALM 27:14

Wait for the LORD; be strong and take heart and wait for the LORD.

PSALM 31:19–20, 24

How great is your goodness, which you have stored up for those who fear you, which you bestow in the sight of men on those who take refuge in you. In the shelter of your presence you hide them from the intrigues of men; in your dwelling you keep them safe from accusing tongues. Be strong and take heart, all you who hope in the LORD.

ISAIAH 54:4

Do not be afraid; you will not suffer shame. Do not fear disgrace; you will not be humiliated. You will forget the shame of your youth and remember no more the reproach of your widowhood.

ISAIAH 41:10–13
Do not fear, for I am with you; do not be
dismayed, for I am your God. I will
strengthen you and help you; I will
uphold you with my righteous right hand.
All who rage against you will surely be
ashamed and disgraced; those who oppose
you will be as nothing and perish. Though
you search for your enemies, you will not
find them. Those who wage war against
you will be as nothing at all. For I am the
LORD, your God, who takes hold of your
right hand and says to you, Do not fear; I
will help you.

JOSHUA 1:9
Be strong and courageous. Do not be terrified;
do not be discouraged, for the LORD your God
will be with you wherever you go.

DEUTERONOMY 31:6, 8
Be strong and courageous. Do not be
afraid or terrified because of them, for
the LORD your God goes with you; he
will never leave you nor forsake you.
The LORD himself goes before you
and will be with you; he will never
leave you nor forsake you. Do not be
afraid; do not be discouraged.

2 TIMOTHY 1:7
For God did not give us a spirit of timidity, but a spirit of power, of love
and of self-discipline.

A LETTER TO *Heaven*

Dear Father in Heaven,

I am eagerly writing to You about something I want to grow in and have a deeper understanding of. To me, love is the ultimate wonder, yet it is also the most completely confounding mystery of all. There are times I seem to excel in even the deepest forms of love. At those times I am the very person I always thought I could be. Then there are the times when my own selfishness barges in through the door of my heart like an unwanted intruder, and I cannot seem to assemble even the smallest affection. My eyes narrow, and I look at others with criticism rather than concern and cool suspicion rather than inviting trust. At those times I am much less than the person I long to be.

You love so completely and compassionately. You love the failure as well as the fulfilled, the faint as well as the forceful, the frail as well as the strong. You are able to love me when I am overflowing with love as well as when I am selfish and small. I need Your words of warmth and wisdom and promise to fill me every day and in every way so that Your love lives in me and is felt by all those I encounter. Help me to love as You do, and make me more consistently the person I've always known I could be.

Your Loving Child

A LETTER FROM *Heaven*

Dear Child of Mine,

I want you to grasp hold of My love—how wide and long, how high and deep it is. The magnitude of true love can be confounding because it surpasses human knowledge. However, when you are able to live a life of love, you will be filled with all of My fullness. For you see, I am love, and when you love Me and live a life of love, I live in you.

The whole reason you are able to love is because I first loved you. Now, you must love others just as I have loved you. When you do, you will be patient and kind. You will not be jealous or boastful or proud. You will not be rude, selfish, or short-tempered. You won't add up the failures of others. Your heart will not find pleasure in evil, but you will enjoy truth. You will always trust, always hope, and always remain strong.

Your Loving Father

from Ephesians 3:17–19; 1 John 4:16, 19
1 Corinthians 13:4–7

God's Word OF PROMISE

JOHN 13:34

A new command I give you: Love one another. As I have loved you, so you must love one another.

JEREMIAH 31:3

The LORD appeared to us in the past, saying: "I have loved you with an everlasting love; I have drawn you with loving-kindness."

EPHESIANS 3:17–19

I pray that you, being rooted and established in love, may have power, together with all the saints, to grasp how wide and long and high and deep is the love of Christ, and to know this love that surpasses knowledge—that you may be filled to the measure of all the fullness of God.

DEUTERONOMY 7:9

Know therefore that the LORD your God is God; he is the faithful God, keeping his covenant of love to a thousand generations of those who love him and keep his commands.

1 JOHN 4:16

And so we know and rely on the love God has for us. God is love. Whoever lives in love lives in God, and God in him.

PSALM 36:5, 7–9
Your love, O LORD, reaches to the heavens, your faithfulness to the skies. How priceless is your unfailing love! Both high and low among men find refuge in the shadow of your wings. They feast on the abundance of your house; you give them drink from your river of delights. For with you is the fountain of life: in your light we see light.

1 JOHN 4:19
We love because he first loved us.

1 CORINTHIANS 13:4–7
Love is patient, love is kind. It does not envy, it does not boast, it is not proud. It is not rude, it is not self-seeking, it is not easily angered, it keeps no record of wrongs. Love does not delight in evil but rejoices with the truth. It always protects, always trusts, always hopes, always perseveres.

A LETTER TO *Heaven*

Dear Father,

Today, I need the promise of Your strength. I have looked ahead at my near future and what I see will take a heavenly strength and a heart of commitment I am not sure I possess. I am already feeling the temptation to compromise on some of my convictions and lower standards I know must be held high.

It is not a question of Your power. I know that Your superior strength has stood the tests of time and trial. Your own unwavering commitment to love me has been tested by doubt and defiance, and not once has it ever failed to deliver its gentle touch or firm discipline when needed. Your patience has been stretched by disobedience and deception, and it has always covered every corner of human life. No, it is certainly not Your strength that I question; it is mine. I do not want my frailties to fail You in the heat of daily battles or when confronting colossal calamities that everyone endures at some time in life. I am turning to You to give me Your strength for today, tomorrow, and forever.

Your Devoted Child

A LETTER FROM *Heaven*

Dear Devoted One,

You are right to come to Me when you are weary and feel the weight of many concerns because you know I will put your heart to rest. Hear My teachings and take them into your heart, and you will find rest from what troubles you. I am your protection and your strength. I will always help you when the times of trouble come. You can say to yourself, "The Lord all powerful is with us, and He is our defender."

Not only will I be with you, I will give you strength when you are tired and more power than you need when you are weak. When you trust Me, you will become strong again. In fact, you will rise up like a soaring eagle, run without needing to rest, and you will walk without becoming tired.

Finally, be strong in My immense power. Wear My words like armor, because your struggle isn't with this world but with the unseen forces of evil. Stand your ground using My truth as a belt and my righteousness as protection for your heart, and wear My good news of peace on your feet for readiness and speed. And don't forget your shield of faith, because with it you can douse the flaming arrows that will be thrown at you. Protect your mind with My promised salvation, and always have your sharp sword of the Spirit, which is My Word. One more thing you should do and never quit doing is pray, pray, and pray some more.

Your Father Who Strengthens You   *from Matthew 11:28–30; Psalm 46:1, 11*
Isaiah 40:29, 31; Ephesians 6:10–18

God's Word OF PROMISE

PSALM 46:1, 11

God is our refuge and strength, an ever-present help in trouble. The LORD Almighty is with us; the God of Jacob is our fortress.

MATTHEW 11:28–30

Come to me, all you who are weary and burdened, and I will give you rest. Take my yoke upon you and learn from me, for I am gentle and humble in heart, and you will find rest for your souls. For my yoke is easy and my burden is light.

PSALM 28:7

The LORD is my strength and my shield; my heart trusts in him, and I am helped. My heart leaps for joy and I will give thanks to him in song.

ISAIAH 40:29, 31

He gives strength to the weary and increases the power of the weak. Those who hope in the LORD will renew their strength. They will soar on wings like eagles; they will run and not grow weary, they will walk and not be faint.

PSALM 46:1–3, 10

God is our refuge and strength, an ever-present help in trouble. Therefore we will not fear, though the earth give way and the mountains fall into the heart of the sea, though its waters roar and foam and the mountains quake with their surging. Be still, and know that I am God.

PSALM 18:32–33, 35

It is God who arms me with strength and makes my way perfect. He makes my feet like the feet of a deer; he enables me to stand on the heights. You give me your shield of victory, and your right hand sustains me; you stoop down to make me great.

EPHESIANS 6:10–18
Finally, be strong in the Lord and in his mighty power. Put on the full armor of God so that you can take your stand against the devil's schemes. For our struggle is not against flesh and blood, but against the rulers, against the authorities, against the powers of this dark world and against the spiritual forces of evil in the heavenly realms. Therefore put on the full armor of God, so that when the day of evil comes, you may be able to stand your ground, and after you have done everything, to stand. Stand firm then, with the belt of truth buckled around your waist, with the breastplate of righteousness in place, and with your feet fitted with the readiness that comes from the gospel of peace. In addition to all this, take up the shield of faith, with which you can extinguish all the flaming arrows of the evil one. Take the helmet of salvation and the sword of the Spirit, which is the word of God. And pray in the Spirit on all occasions with all kinds of prayers and requests. With this in mind, be alert and always keep on praying for all the saints.

1 CHRONICLES 16:11
Look to the LORD and his strength; seek his face always.

A LETTER TO *Heaven*

Dear Father,

What I am writing You about has become a serious problem that only You can help me with. I've thought about talking to others about it, but there is no one who has the answer to this but You. I am feeling unforgiven. It has become so serious that my bones ache, my vision is fading, and sometimes I awaken in tears for no apparent reason. My future seems bleak because my present is dark with doom and despair.

It is not one simple failure that has caused me to stumble. Instead, I seem to have accumulated my sins into a mountain that blocks my vision of Your mercy. Your words have always been filled with faithful mercy, and I need to hear You now. Your words will be received like a refreshing rain to my soul. Send Your words quickly. I thirst for the freedom of Your forgiveness.

Your Child Who Seeks Assurance

A LETTER FROM *Heaven*

My Dear Child,

I have received your request, and here is My prompt response. If you, My child called by My name, will humble yourself, pray, pursue Me, and turn your back on any evil thing you encounter, I will hear you in heaven and will send forgiveness and healing to you. You can trust that when you confess your mistakes and misdeeds, I will forgive you and even wash you clean from those things that have made you feel unforgiven.

Though your mistakes have deeply colored your life, you can once again be white as wintry snow. Though your missteps have stained your life and conscience, I can make you pure again. If you do not condemn others, you will not be condemned. If you forgive, you will be forgiven; if you give, it will be given back. In fact, I will shake together and stuff so many blessings that they will overflow and pour right into your lap.

Be happy when you are forgiven and your past is pardoned. Feel blessed, for I will not find you guilty when you are truthful and trustworthy.

Your Loving Father

from 2 Chronicles 7:12, 14; 1 John 1:9
Isaiah 1:18; Luke 6:35–38; Psalm 32:1–2

God's Word OF PROMISE

2 CHRONICLES 7:12, 14
I have heard your prayer and have chosen this place for myself as a temple for sacrifices. If my people, who are called by my name, will humble themselves and pray and seek my face and turn from their wicked ways, then will I hear from heaven and will forgive their sin and will heal their land.

ISAIAH 43:25
I, even I, am he who blots out your transgressions, for my own sake, and remembers your sins no more.

PSALM 103:12
As far as the east is from the west, so far has he removed our transgressions from us.

1 JOHN 1:9
If we confess our sins, he is faithful and just and will forgive us our sins and purify us from all unrighteousness.

PSALM 32:1–2
Blessed is he whose transgressions are forgiven, whose sins are covered. Blessed is the man whose sin the LORD does not count against him and in whose spirit is no deceit.

ISAIAH 1:18
"Come now, let us reason together," says the LORD. "Though your sins are like scarlet, they shall be as white as snow; though they are red as crimson, they shall be like wool."

1 JOHN 3:19–20
This then is how we know that we belong to the truth, and how we set our hearts at rest in his presence whenever our hearts condemn us. For God is greater than our hearts, and he knows everything.

LUKE 6:35–38
But love your enemies, do good to them, and lend to them without expecting to get anything back. Then your reward will be great, and you will be sons of the Most High, because he is kind to the ungrateful and wicked. Be merciful, just as your Father is merciful. Do not judge, and you will not be judged. Do not condemn, and you will not be condemned. Forgive, and you will be forgiven. Give, and it will be given to you. A good measure, pressed down, shaken together and running over, will be poured into your lap. For with the measure you use, it will be measured to you.

A LETTER TO *Heaven*

Dear Father of Comfort,

Please receive this message with urgency and respond quickly. My heart is aching, and my spirit is broken from wounds that are so deep they can't be seen by human eyes. That is why I have run to You. I knew You could see them and would bring me the comfort I seek and so desperately need. Something happened, something wrong and disturbing, and it has left me sad, hurt, and heartbroken. I am unable to find my way through this storm, and I need to feel the warmth of Your light again.

I know others have noticed it, because of my fallen countenance. My friends have made efforts to cheer me up, but I need more. I remember the comfort You supplied to Hannah in her heartbreak, to David in his depression, and to Joseph in the injustice done to him. There was the widow who lost her son and the countless others whose lives You have calmed with Your comfort and understanding.

Speak to me Your promise of comfort; breathe on me the soothing winds of Your understanding. I eagerly anticipate Your response.

Your Hurting Child

A LETTER FROM *Heaven*

Dear Hurting Child,

I am glad you came to Me because I am full of mercy and comfort. I will comfort you every time you are troubled. I do it not only for your sake but so you can bring that same comfort to others. I will comfort you as a mother comforts her child. You will be able to shout for joy and even burst out in song because of the comfort and compassion that I bring to My injured children.

Think of Me as a good and solid shelter in your times of trouble, for I feel deeply the pains of those who trust Me. Yes, I'll be your refuge and strength and constant companion in your struggles. You don't need to be afraid even when the world gives way or the mountains crumble into the ocean or when the storm-tossed sea and the quaking earth threaten your security. Even when you walk through a dark valley, you will not need to be afraid, because My rod and walking stick will comfort you.

I have told you these things so that in Me you can experience peace. There is trouble in this world, but be strong because I have overcome the world. Don't forget what I have promised you: I will never leave you or forget you.

Your Father of Comfort

from 1 Corinthians 1:3–5; Isaiah 66:13; 49:13
Nahum 1:7; Psalms 46:1–3; 23:4
John 16:33; Hebrews 13:5

God's Word OF PROMISE

ISAIAH 49:13

Shout for joy, O heavens; rejoice,
O earth; burst into song, O mountains! For the
LORD comforts his people and will have compassion
on his afflicted ones.

ISAIAH 66:13

As a mother comforts her child, so will I comfort
you; and you will be comforted over Jerusalem.

1 CORINTHIANS 1:3–5

Grace and peace to you from God
our Father and the Lord Jesus
Christ. I always thank God for you
because of his grace given you in
Christ Jesus. For in him you have
been enriched in every way—in all
your speaking and in all your
knowledge.

NAHUM 1:7

The LORD is good, a refuge in times of trouble. He
cares for those who trust in him.

PSALM 23:4
Even though I walk through the valley of the
shadow of death, I will fear no evil, for you are with me; your
rod and your staff, they comfort me.

PSALM 46:1–3
God is our refuge and strength, an ever-present help in
trouble. Therefore we will not fear, though the earth
give way and the mountains fall into the heart of the
sea, though its waters roar and foam and the mountains quake with their surging.

JOHN 16:33
I have told you these
things, so that in me
you may have peace.
In this world you will
have trouble. But take
heart! I have overcome
the world.

HEBREWS 13:5
Never will I leave you; never
will I forsake you.

A LETTER TO *Heaven*

Dear God of Patience,

I am so glad You are patient, and right now I wish I were too. This problem has deeply affected my family—the very people I ought to have the most patience with. When something doesn't go smoothly with them, I become entirely too short-tempered and short-sighted. I've also become irritable with coworkers who can't seem to accomplish their tasks quickly enough or flawlessly enough to please me. I care about these people, but You wouldn't know it by the way I've been behaving toward them. If that's not bad enough, I actually became upset with a fax machine recently because I thought it should work faster.

But the worst part of all is that I have grown impatient with You. I'm ashamed to say it, but it's true. There are certain elements of my life and myself I want big changes in. I have prayed hard about them, but everything remains the same. I want my life to change yesterday rather than tomorrow, and I want my troubles to go away immediately and to take my weaknesses with them.

Now, I'm simply praying for patience, and not just normal everyday patience, but the heavenly kind—the kind that says I love my family, friends, and coworkers, the kind that allows myself to make mistakes and the time to transform character flaws. I especially desire the kind that waits on You with total trust and confidence. In other words, I want a patience like Yours.

Your Impatient Child

A LETTER FROM *Heaven*

Dearest Impatient Child,

You have been thinking about your trials and tensions all wrong. You should regard these many trials with unadulterated joy, because you know that it is these very troubles that will result in your gaining the patience you desire. Then this patience will produce the character you hope to have; in turn, that character produces more hope—a hope that never disappoints because I have poured out My love so much that it fills your very heart. Consider the example of the farmer who waits patiently on the land until it gives him a crop; note how patient he is in waiting for the rain to come.

As you are waiting, you should always pray and not give up. Then you will call out for Me and come and pray to Me, and you can be sure that I will listen. Call on Me when you are in trouble: I will rescue you, and then you will bring Me honor. Do not become discouraged in doing good things, for you can be sure that they will produce fruit at just the right time. Grasp hold of the hope that you talk about and never let go, knowing I have promised and I am faithful.

Your Patient and Long-Suffering Father

from James 1:2–4; Romans 5:3; James 5:7–8
Luke 18:1; Jeremiah 29:12; Galatians 6:9

God's Word OF PROMISE

HEBREWS 10:36

You need to persevere so that when you have done the will of God, you will receive what he has promised.

ROMANS 5:3–4

We also rejoice in our sufferings, because we know that suffering produces perseverance; perseverance, character; and character, hope.

JAMES 5:7–8

Be patient, then, brothers, until the Lord's coming. See how the farmer waits for the land to yield its valuable crop and how patient he is for the autumn and spring rains. You too, be patient and stand firm, because the Lord's coming is near.

JEREMIAH 29:12

Then you will call upon me and come and pray to me, and I will listen to you.

GALATIANS 6:9
Let us not become weary in doing good, for at the proper time we will reap a harvest if we do not give up.

JAMES 1:2–4
Consider it pure joy, my brothers, whenever you face trials of many kinds, because you know that the testing of your faith develops perseverance. Perseverance must finish its work so that you may be mature and complete, not lacking anything.

LUKE 18:1
Then Jesus told his disciples a parable to show them that they should always pray and not give up.

A LETTER TO *Heaven*

Dear God of Guidance,

I have been making plans lately and writing down goals. Things I would very much like to achieve and places I want to go. Then it struck me. Can I get there by myself, can I define my desires, pursue my plans, or reach my destinations without Your guidance? Is it possible for me to reach the peaks, sit on the summits, see the sunsets, or climb the cavernous walls without Your direction? I answered my own questions with a resounding *no*. I can't even see tomorrow's sunrise. How can I detail the path to my own life's sunset?

There are dangers ahead I cannot detect and storms I cannot forecast. That is what brings me to You. I need to feel Your strong hand grasping mine so that when I stumble I will not fall. Lead me with steps that will not be too large for my legs, to destinations that will not be too far for me to reach, and to depths I can only dream of. You know me better than I know myself. You know what I am capable of—what I am too weak to climb, too blind to see, and too proud to admit. I will not go anywhere without You. I would not get there even if I tried.

Your Faithful Follower

A LETTER FROM *Heaven*

Dear Faithful Follower,

It is true that people make many plans and outline them in their minds, but you know that only I can make them a reality. When you rely on Me in whatever you do, your plans will succeed. When people say "Today or tomorrow we will go here, build a business, and make lots of money," they don't know what they are saying. They don't even know what will happen tomorrow. Whether you go right or left, you are going to hear My voice saying "This is the way, walk in it."

I will constantly lead you and will supply your needs in barren times, and I will strengthen your bones. You will be like a garden that is always being watered and like a spring that never runs dry. In everything you do, simply recognize Me, and I will make sure the road you're on is straight. I am committed to instructing you and teaching you in which way you should go. I will advise you and protect you.

I will turn darkness into light right in front of you and will make rough places smooth. These are the things I will do, and I will not fail you.

Your Guiding Father

from Proverbs 16:1, 3; James 4:13–14; Isaiah 30:21; 58:11
Proverbs 3:6; Psalm 32:8; Isaiah 42:16

God's Word OF PROMISE

PROVERBS 16:1, 3
To man belong the plans of the heart, but from the LORD comes the reply of the tongue. Commit to the LORD whatever you do, and your plans will succeed.

JAMES 4:13–14
Now listen, you who say, "Today or tomorrow we will go to this or that city, spend a year there, carry on business and make money." Why, you do not even know what will happen tomorrow.

ISAIAH 30:21
Whether you turn to the right or to the left, your ears will hear a voice behind you, saying, "This is the way: walk in it."

PROVERBS 3:6
In all your ways acknowledge him, and he will make your paths straight.

ISAIAH 42:16
I will lead the blind by ways they have not known, along unfamiliar paths I will guide them; I will turn the darkness into light before them and make the rough places smooth. These are the things I will do; I will not forsake them.

ISAIAH 58:11
The LORD will guide you always; he will satisfy your needs in a sun-scorched land and will strengthen your frame. You will be like a well-watered garden, like a spring whose waters never fail.

PSALM 32:8
I will instruct you and teach you in the way you should go; I will counsel you and watch over you.

A LETTER TO *Heaven*

Dear God of Love,

I have figured something out, and I wanted to let You know right away. It won't be a surprise to You, but it seems I need to be reminded of it from time to time. Your love is what I need more than anything else. I told You it wouldn't be a surprise to You. And do You know what else I discovered? I like it that way.

It is absolutely wonderful to know that when I fail, and I do quite often, I can curl up in Your assuring embrace so that I can forgive myself and leave the guilt behind. When I am wounded, Your love comes quickly to soothe the pain and quicken my healing. When I am running the race of life every day, Your loving voice encourages me on to the finish. It's great to know that because of Your devotion, I'm always considered a winner. Your love is full of the protection I need, the power I depend on, and the promise that sustains me. There is something else I wanted to tell You too. I love You.

Your Dearly Loved Child

A LETTER FROM *Heaven*

Dearly Loved Child,

I have loved you with an eternal love; I have pulled you close with loving-kindness. In all things, you are more than a winner through My love. There is nothing in all creation that will separate you from My love—not death or life, not angels or demons, not the present, the future, or any other power. May you, being firmly planted and formed in love, have power, with all of My children, to comprehend just how wide and long and high and deep is the love of Christ. And may you know this love—that absolutely goes beyond human knowledge—so that you may be filled to the fullest with all of My fullness.

In a race, all the runners run, but only one gets the prize. Run to win the prize. I am with you, and I am strong enough to save. I take great pride in you. I will calm you with love and rejoice over you with singing. Remember what is written: "No eye has seen, no ear has heard, no mind has conceived what I have prepared for those who love me."

Your Loving and Devoted God

from Jeremiah 31:3; Romans 8:37–39
Ephesians 3:17–19; 1 Corinthians 9:24; Zephaniah 3:17

God's Word OF PROMISE

ZEPHANIAH 3:17
The LORD your God is with you, he is mighty to save. He will take great delight in you, he will quiet you with his love, he will rejoice over you with singing.

EPHESIANS 3:17–19
I pray that you, being rooted and established in love, may have power, together with all the saints, to grasp how wide and long and high and deep is the love of Christ, and to know this love that surpasses knowledge—that you may be filled to the measure of all the fullness of God.

JEREMIAH 31:3
The LORD appeared to us in the past, saying: "I have loved you with an everlasting love; I have drawn you with loving-kindness."

1 CORINTHIANS 9:24
Do you not know that in a race all the runners run, but only one gets the prize? Run in such a way as to get the prize.

1 Corinthians 2:9
No eye has seen, no ear has
heard, no mind has conceived
what God has prepared for
those who love him.

Romans 8:37–39
In all these things we are more
than conquerors through him who
loved us. For I am convinced that
neither death nor life, neither
angels nor demons, neither the
present nor the future, nor any
powers, neither height nor depth,
nor anything else in all creation,
will be able to separate us from
the love of God that is in Christ
Jesus our Lord.

1 John 4:16
And so we know and rely on the love God has for us.
God is love. Whoever lives in love lives in God, and
God in him.

Jeremiah 32:41
I will rejoice in doing them good
and will assuredly plant them in
this land with all my heart and
soul.

A LETTER TO *Heaven*

Dear Father in Heaven,

I know You have been good to me. I do not really lack anything in my life. I have food, a warm place to live and sleep, and I have friends and family. That's why I am more than a little troubled by the discontent I feel growing within me. It's like a splinter that has been lodged in my heart. It seems I have unknowingly picked it up somewhere. It has become inflamed and enlarged and is an irritation that I want removed.

I have noticed that I am beginning to look at what others *have* instead of what others *are*. It seems that I count what I don't possess rather than relish the gifts and blessings I do. Even as I sense these desires growing and contentment fading, I live with a keen awareness that the accumulation of things only leaves a hunger for more rather than a peaceful satisfaction. This cannot be good. It can only lead to heartache and disappointment. Ultimately, it will tear at my relationships and my real ambitions, and it will paralyze my ability to accomplish the things that endure and to gather and save that which has eternal value. Please help me dissuade my heart from craving the carnal rather than hungering for the heavenly. Your words of promise will satisfy my desires and dislodge this splinter of discontent.

Your Discontented Child

A LETTER FROM *Heaven*

Dear Child of Mine,

Don't let trouble overtake your heart; trust in Me. Free yourself from the love of money, and find contentment in what you have, knowing that I will not leave you or fail you. Therefore, you don't have to worry about your life, what you will eat or drink, or even about you will wear on your body. After all, isn't life a great deal more important than what you will eat and your body more important than the clothes you put on it? Of course they are.

I want you to think for a minute about the birds: They don't work a job or accumulate anything, and yet I feed them. Aren't you much more important to Me than they are? And what about clothes? Look at the flowers in the field. They don't work for a living. Yet I am telling you that not even Solomon in his very best possessed such beauty and brilliance.

Don't attempt to make or save a fortune for yourself while you're here on earth because it will all be destroyed one way or another, or it might be stolen by a thief. Make your fortune in heaven, where it can never be stolen or destroyed.

Remember this, you gain a great deal when you possess both godliness and contentment. When you were born, you brought nothing with you, and when you leave this earth, you will take nothing with you.

Your Great Provider

from John 14:1; Hebrews 13:5; Matthew 6:25–29, 19–21
Proverbs 14:30; 1 Timothy 6:6

God's Word OF PROMISE

HEBREWS 13:5
Keep your lives free from the love of money and be content with what you have, because God has said, "Never will I leave you; never will I forsake you."

1 TIMOTHY 6:6
But godliness with contentment is great gain.

PROVERBS 14:30
A heart at peace gives life to the body, but envy rots the bones.

JOHN 14:1
Do not let your hearts be troubled. Trust in God; trust also in me.

MATTHEW 6:19–21
Do not store up for yourselves treasures on earth, where moth and rust destroy, and where thieves break in and steal. But store up for yourselves treasures in heaven, where moth and rust do not destroy, and where thieves do not break in and steal. For where your treasure is, there your heart will be also.

PHILIPPIANS 4:6–7
Do not be anxious about anything, but in everything, by prayer and petition, with thanksgiving, present your requests to God. And the peace of God, which transcends all understanding, will guard your hearts and your minds in Christ Jesus.

PSALM 85:8
I will listen to what God the Lord will say; he promises peace to his people, his saints.

MATTHEW 6:25–29
Therefore I tell you, do not worry about your life, what you will eat or drink; or about your body, what you will wear. Is not life more important than food, and the body more important than clothes? Look at the birds of the air; they do not sow or reap or store away in barns, and yet your heavenly Father feeds them. Are you not much more valuable than they? Who of you by worrying can add a single hour to his life? And why do you worry about clothes? See how the lilies of the field grow. They do not labor or spin. Yet I tell you that not even Solomon in all his splendor was dressed like one of these.

A *Letter* to *Heaven*

Dear Father of Power,

I have been examining my life, and it seems I can see too much of me and too little of You. It has caused me to request something quite spectacular from You. I want to experience more of Your awesome power in every aspect of my life. I am moved and inspired at how You reveal Your power every day in the grandeur of Your creation and the depth of Your artistry. Everything from the stunning peaks of the tallest mountains to the mysterious depths of the deepest oceans bears Your signature of power.

When the storm rages, the winds blow, and the lightning streaks across the sky, it is Your thunderous voice that is heard heralding Your living power. Your powerful artistry is expressed in the excitement of Your golden dawns and in the peace of Your rich, pastel sunsets. Just as You reveal Your power in these works of creation, I want You to reveal Your power in my life and fill me with Your love. I want all that I do and all that I am to bear Your signature of power. I want the boldness of my actions to light up the horizons and the weight of my words to be spoken with thunderous truth and of a heavenly heart.

Yes, it is my greatest desire that my life be a portrait of Your power, painted by Your almighty hand.

Your Loving Child

A *L*ETTER FROM *Heaven*

Dear Loving Child,

My answer comes from heaven with the rescuing power of My right hand. Counsel and judgment are Mine, and I have understanding and power. By Me kings reign and rulers pass laws; by Me princes govern and nobles lead on earth. With Me are riches and honor, enduring wealth and prosperity. What I produce in life is better than the purest gold and surpasses the finest silver. Who has measured the waters in His hand or with His hand marked off the heavens? Who has held the earth's dust in a basket or placed the mountains on a scale and the hills on a balance? To whom will you compare Me; who is My equal?

I display the stars one by one and call them by name. Because of My great power and strength, not one of them is missing. I will give strength to you when you are weary and increased power when you are weak. You will fly like an eagle, run without growing tired, and walk without fading in strength. For I am a light and a shield, and I give you benefits and honor; nothing good will be withheld from you when you live in purity; fulfillment is in the life of those who trust Me. You do not possess a spirit of timidity, but a spirit of power, of love, and of self-discipline.

Your Powerful and Devoted Father

from Psalm 20:6; Proverbs 8:14–15, 18–19
Isaiah 40:12, 25–26, 29, 31
Psalm 84:11–12; 2 Timothy 1:7

God's Word OF PROMISE

PSALM 20:6

He answers him from his holy heaven with the saving power of his right hand.

ISAIAH 40:29

He gives strength to the weary and increases the power of the weak.

PSALM 147:5–6

Great is our Lord and mighty in power; his understanding has no limit. The LORD sustains the humble.

ISAIAH 40:12, 25–26, 31

Who has measured the waters in the hollow of his hand, or with the breadth of his hand marked off the heavens? Who has held the dust of the earth in a basket, or weighed the mountains on the scales and the hills in a balance? "To whom will you compare me? Or who is my equal?" says the Holy One. Lift your eyes and look to the heavens: Who created all these? He who brings out the starry host one by one, and calls them each by name. Because of his great power and mighty strength, not one of them is missing. Those who hope in the LORD will renew their strength. They will soar on wings like eagles; they will run and not grow weary, they will walk and not be faint.

PSALM 84:11–12
For the LORD God is a sun and shield; the LORD bestows favor and honor; no good thing does he withhold from those whose walk is blameless. O LORD Almighty, blessed is the man who trusts in you.

PROVERBS 8:14–15, 18–19
Counsel and sound judgment are mine; I have understanding and power. By me kings reign and rulers make laws that are just. With me are riches and honor, enduring wealth and prosperity. My fruit is better than fine gold; what I yield surpasses choice silver.

PROVERBS 18:10
The name of the LORD is a strong tower; the righteous run to it and are safe.

2 TIMOTHY 1:7
For God did not give us a spirit of timidity, but a spirit of power, of love and of self-discipline.

A LETTER TO *Heaven*

Dear Generous God,

I know I have communicated this to You before. Probably when I needed money, I told You how generous I would be if You gave me the amount I wanted. Perhaps it was when I felt as if You had given a great deal to me and I wanted to make an effort to pay You something back. I really do desire to be a more gracious giver.

There have probably been times that I have donated my time and my finances, but whatever I have given in the past has not been sacrificial or satisfying. It has not been a giving that is accompanied by joy or peace.

I have held back in my giving because in the recesses of my heart I have not really believed You would take care of me. I have vainly attempted to collect and save more and more so that I would have to depend upon You less and less. This time when I tell You I want to be a giver, a granter, a contributor, I mean what I say. You have held nothing back, I realize that now, and I want to throw caution and concern out of my heart so that I can be generous and openhanded like You, instead of fearful and closefisted. Share generously with me the promises that will inspire my life to give rather than to be guarded or greedy.

Your Child of Promise

A LETTER FROM *Heaven*

Dear Child of Promise,

Just as you try to excel in everything—in faith, in how you speak, in knowledge, in sincerity, and in love—see that you also become a great giver. Remember this: Whoever gives sparingly will also gather sparingly. You should decide from your heart what you want to give—not reluctantly or because you have to—but because I absolutely love My children to be cheerful in their giving. Through Me, you will experience wealth in all kinds of ways so that you in turn can be generous to others. And the result of your generosity will be more and more thanksgiving given to Me.

I don't want you to be like people who hunger for wealth, because such people fall into temptations, traps, and foolish desires that bring them harm and plunge them into ruin and even destruction. The love of money is the reason all different kinds of evil exists. It has even caused some of My children to wander away, and now their hearts are pierced with grief. I don't want that for you. Don't place any hope in wealth; it is just too uncertain. Place your hope in Me, because I am the great provider. Your job is to concentrate on doing good things, becoming wealthy in good actions, and being generous and sharing. In this way you will accumulate heavenly treasure as a firm foundation for the age to come. Now *that* is living.

Your Giving Father

from 2 Corinthians 8:7; 9:6–8, 11
1 Timothy 6:9–10; 6:17–19

God's Word OF PROMISE

2 CORINTHIANS 8:7

But just as you excel in everything —in faith, in speech, in knowledge, in complete earnestness and in your love for us—see that you also excel in this grace of giving.

PROVERBS 3:9–10

Honor the LORD with your wealth, with the firstfruits of all your crops; then your barns will be filled to overflowing, and your vats will brim over with new wine.

2 CORINTHIANS 9:6–8

Remember this: Whoever sows sparingly will also reap sparingly, and whoever sows generously will also reap generously. Each man should give what he has decided in his heart to give, not reluctantly or under compulsion, for God loves a cheerful giver. And God is able to make all grace abound to you, so that in all things at all times, having all that you need, you will abound in every good work.

MALACHI 3:10

"Bring the whole tithe into the storehouse, that there may be food in my house. Test me in this," says the LORD Almighty, "and see if I will not throw open the floodgates of heaven and pour out so much blessing that you will not have room enough for it."

2 CORINTHIANS 9:11

You will be made rich in every way so that you can be generous on every occasion, and through us your generosity will result in thanksgiving to God.

1 TIMOTHY 6:9–10

People who want to get rich fall into temptation and a trap and into many foolish and harmful desires that plunge men into ruin and destruction. For the love of money is a root of all kinds of evil. Some people, eager for money, have wandered from the faith and pierced themselves with many griefs.

1 TIMOTHY 6:17–19

Command those who are rich in this present world not to be arrogant nor to put their hope in wealth, which is so uncertain, but to put their hope in God, who richly provides us with everything for our enjoyment. Command them to do good, to be rich in good deeds, and to be generous and willing to share. In this way they will lay up treasure for themselves as a firm foundation for the coming age, so that they may take hold of the life that is truly life.

LUKE 6:38

Give, and it will be given to you. A good measure, pressed down, shaken together and running over, will be poured into your lap. For with the measure you use, it will be measured to you.

A Letter to *Heaven*

Dear God,

I am writing to You about something that seems like it ought to be easy to overcome, but I am having great difficulty with it. I am being nagged by a mysterious kind of loneliness. I know the answer should be obvious: I should go to church, get with friends, and stay close to my family. I've done all that, and I am still consumed by this uneasy isolation. Even though no one has said the words or pushed me away, I still feel somehow rejected. I've begun to wonder if anyone really cares what I face every day, what frustrates me, fuels my anger, or feeds my soul. I don't really feel a part of anyone on an intimate basis where we are able to share heartaches, hassles, celebrations, and triumphs.

I want to be able to wrap my life with the lives of others so that together we might function as a single heart. I hunger for relationships that hope for the best, hold each other up, share one another's sadness, and cheer each victory in the arena of daily conflict. I want forgiveness to be plentiful, failures to find understanding, and needs to be aggressively met.

And above all, I want this loneliness to leave me and never return, for it makes me feel distant even from You. I love You, I love people, and I need to be assured of Your love and the love of others.

Your Devoted Child

A LETTER FROM *Heaven*

Dear Child,

I am not a God who is distant from you, but rather I am always very close-by. Come near to Me and I will come near to You. When you call, I will answer; when you cry for help, I will respond by saying, "Here I am." You are precious and honored in My eyes, and I truly love you. I will never leave you or fail you. I am a Father to you, and you are My child. I am with you and will look out for you wherever you go.

The most important thing I have told you to do is to love Me with all of your heart and then to love your friends and family as much as you love yourself. You can't do anything more important than this. That love must be the most sincere kind, and sincere love hates evil and holds tightly to what is good. Be devoted to others with a brotherly love. Honor and admire others above yourself. Never let your enthusiasm fade away, but keep your intensity burning in support of Me.

Delight yourself with hope; be patient even when you are wounded and unwavering in your prayer life. How pleasant life is when my children live as one. Do everything necessary to maintain unity in the Spirit through the bond of peace. Put up with others, and forgive whatever you may be holding against them. Forgive, just like I have forgiven you. And you can be sure that I will be right there with you even until the end of time.

Your God Who Is Always Near

from Deuteronomy 31:6; 2 Corinthians 6:18
Genesis 28:15; Mark 12:29–31; Romans 12:9–12
Psalm 133:1; Ephesians 4:3; Matthew 28:20
James 4:8; Isaiah 58:9; 43:4

47

God's Word OF PROMISE

ISAIAH 43:4
Since you are precious and
honored in my sight, and because I love
you, I will give men in exchange for you,
and people in exchange for your life.

2 CORINTHIANS 6:18
"I will be a Father to you,
and you will be my sons and
daughters," says the Lord
Almighty.

DEUTERONOMY 31:6
Be strong and courageous. Do not be afraid or terrified because of them, for the
LORD your God goes with you; he will never leave you nor forsake you.

JAMES 4:8
Come near to God and he will
come near to you.

ISAIAH 58:9
Then you will call,
and the LORD will
answer; you will
cry for help, and he
will say: Here am I.

MARK 12:29–31
"The most important one," answered Jesus, "is this: 'Hear, O
Israel, the Lord our God, the Lord is one. Love the Lord your
God with all your heart and with all your soul and with all your
mind and with all your strength.' The second is this: 'Love your
neighbor as yourself.' There is no commandment greater than
these."

COLOSSIANS 3:12–14
Therefore, as God's chosen people, holy and dearly loved, clothe yourselves with compassion, kindness, humility, gentleness and patience. Bear with each other and forgive whatever grievances you may have against one another. Forgive as the Lord forgave you. And over all these virtues put on love, which binds them all together in perfect unity.

ROMANS 12:9–12
Love must be sincere. Hate what is evil; cling to what is good. Be devoted to one another in brotherly love. Honor one another above yourselves. Never be lacking in zeal, but keep your spiritual fervor, serving the Lord. Be joyful in hope, patient in affliction, faithful in prayer.

EPHESIANS 4:3
Make every effort to keep the unity of the Spirit through the bond of peace.

PSALM 133:1
How good and pleasant it is when brothers live together in unity!

GENESIS 28:15
I am with you and will watch over you wherever you go, and I will bring you back to this land.

MATTHEW 28:20
And surely I am with you always, to the very end of the age.

49

A LETTER TO *Heaven*

Dear Father in Heaven,

It's me again, but of course You already knew that I would be writing. You know every-thing about me—my likes, dislikes, desires, and (though I wish You didn't) my deepest secrets. That's why I'm writing. I made a mistake, and rather than come to You about it, I have tried to hide it in a secret place in my heart and repair the damage on my own. I don't know why I tried to bury it behind a wall of denial, but I did.

Then the truth swept into my soul like a storm and reminded me that I could never keep my frailties or failures concealed from Your sight. What in all creation are You not aware of? You see the sun rising and setting on the earth with one glance. You send the winds that sing through the pines on mountain peaks, pour out the rain on parched fields, and smile at ocean waves as they powerfully pound against the rocks and boldly pronounce Your greatness. You hear the cries of the crushed and feel the pain of the fallen; You raise Your hands and cheer Your children on to victory.

So now I come, dropping my disguises and asking You, in full view of my mistake, to grant me forgiveness and help me in righting this wrong. Help me cleanse my heart, and bring a healing hand to any and all that I have hurt. Send Your response quickly.

Your Apologetic Child

A *L*ETTER FROM *Heaven*

Dear Apologetic Child,

There are rich blessings for those whose failures find forgiveness and whose mistakes are covered. Happiness belongs to those whose sin I cannot find and in whose soul there is no deceit. When you keep silent about sin, your body will weaken and your heart will constantly groan with sadness. Acknowledge your mistakes and confess your faults, and you will find forgiveness and freedom from guilt. If you hide your failures, you will have no success. If you openly confess and turn away from the wrong, you will receive mercy.

I am going to teach you what to do and where to go from here; I will counsel you and protect you. Do not resist Me like a rebellious horse or mule that has to be led around by the nose. Those who are corrupt live in exceeding sadness, but My unfailing love surrounds the one who trusts Me. Confess your sins and pray that you may experience healing. The prayer offered by a person who has been made right is powerful and effective. Do not repay evil with evil, but be careful to do the right thing in plain sight of everyone. If at all possible, live in peace with everyone. From now on, do the things that lead to peace and that bring blessings not only to yourself but also to everyone else.

Your Understanding Father in Heaven

from Psalm 32:1–5; Proverbs 28:13; Psalm 32:8–10
James 5:16; Romans 12:17–18; 14:19

God's Word OF PROMISE

ROMANS 14:19
Let us therefore make every effort to do what leads to peace and to mutual edification.

PSALM 32:8–10
I will instruct you and teach you in the way you should go; I will counsel you and watch over you. Do not be like the horse or the mule, which have no understanding but must be controlled by bit and bridle or they will not come to you. Many are the woes of the wicked, but the LORD'S unfailing love surrounds the man who trusts in him.

JEREMIAH 33:3
Call to me and I will answer you and tell you great and unsearchable things you do not know.

PROVERBS 28:13
He who conceals his sins does not prosper, but whoever confesses and renounces them finds mercy.

JAMES 5:16

Therefore confess your sins to each other and pray for each other so that you may be healed. The prayer of a righteous man is powerful and effective.

PSALM 32:1–5

Blessed is he whose transgressions are forgiven, whose sins are covered. Blessed is the man whose sin the LORD does not count against him and in whose spirit is no deceit. When I kept silent, my bones wasted away through my groaning all day long. For day and night your hand was heavy upon me; my strength was sapped as in the heat of summer. Then I acknowledged my sin to you and did not cover up my iniquity. I said, "I will confess my transgressions to the LORD"—and you forgave the guilt of my sin.

ROMANS 12:17–18

Do not repay anyone evil for evil. Be careful to do what is right in the eyes of everybody. If it is possible, as far as it depends on you, live at peace with everyone.

A LETTER TO *Heaven*

Dear God,

What happened to my plans? They seemed so right, but absolutely everything went wrong. I am writing this with a little anger, a bit of confusion, and a lot of disappointment. I was so certain that the plans I had made and the prayers I offered would be answered by You. I was sure that You would work out the problems, walk with me down the path, and help me win the prize I was pursuing. But You didn't.

I found myself at the end of my dreams, empty-handed and brokenhearted. There must be a reason. You must have seen something I couldn't. Was there a danger in my plans that would have damaged my life? Was there pain or loss I could not withstand? Were there cracks in the foundation of my future that would have collapsed the walls around me?

I must know, because I believed so much in the dreams, that disappointment now haunts me. I fear daring to dream again. You are my hope and future. I long to hear Your answer.

Your Disappointed Child

A *L*ETTER FROM *Heaven*

Dear Disappointed Child,

I want you to trust Me with all your heart and not to depend on your own understanding. Along with your trust, I want you to acknowledge Me in everything you do, and I will make certain the path you choose is straight. Find your fulfillment in Me, and I will give you what your heart really desires. Continue to pledge your plans to Me and trust Me, and I will do it. You must understand that you might choose a way that seems absolutely right to you but will end in death.

I am going to keep you from getting badly hurt, and I will watch over your whole life. I will keep a close watch on everything you do all the days of your life and beyond. Hear My words: My thinking about things is different from your thinking. Your ways are not the same as Mine. My thinking and ways are as far from yours as the earth is from the sky. Even though you may have disappointment now, you will be happy because I will comfort you. When you hunger to do right more than anything else, you will be happy, because I will completely satisfy you. I am your sun and shield; I give favor and honor; there is not one good thing that I will keep from you when you walk blamelessly. Those who trust in Me will be blessed.

Your God of Grace

from Proverbs 3:5–6; Psalm 37:4–5; Proverbs 14:12
Psalm 121:7–8; Isaiah 55:8–9; Matthew 5:4, 6
Psalm 84:11–12

God's Word OF PROMISE

PSALM 37:4–5

Delight yourself in the LORD and he
will give you the desires of your heart.
Commit your way to the LORD; trust in
him and he will do this: He will make
your righteousness shine like the
dawn, the justice of your cause like
the noonday sun.

PROVERBS 3:5–6

Trust in the LORD with all your
heart and lean not on your own
understanding; in all your ways
acknowledge him, and he will
make your paths straight.

MATTHEW 5:4, 6

Blessed are those who
mourn, for they will be
comforted. Blessed are
those who hunger and
thirst for righteousness,
for they will be filled.

PSALM 84:11–12

For the LORD God is a sun and shield; the LORD bestows favor and honor; no good thing does he withhold from those whose walk is blameless. O LORD Almighty, blessed is the man who trusts in you.

PROVERBS 14:12

There is a way that seems right to a man, but in the end it leads to death.

ISAIAH 55:8–9

"For my thoughts are not your thoughts, neither are your ways my ways," declares the LORD. "As the heavens are higher than the earth, so are my ways higher than your ways and my thoughts than your thoughts."

PSALM 121:7–8

The LORD will keep you from all harm—he will watch over your life; the LORD will watch over your coming and going both now and forevermore.

A LETTER TO *Heaven*

Dear Father,

I really blew it, and I know it. I let my anger out of its cage, and it did some damage. I know that anger never solves anything but, in fact, does a great deal of harm. Believe me when I tell You that if I could relive those few furious moments when I lost control, I would hold my tongue and harbor by temper. As it is, I ended up hurting someone else, and my anger has built a wall that I must tear down.

What was done wasn't deserving of anger; I simply let myself fall into a bad mood on a rough day, and the small thing that was done seemed a hundred times worse than it really was. Without thinking, my emotions jumped from my mouth with words I did not really mean. Before I go and say I'm sorry to the person I hurt, I want to apologize to You.

You have made it known that there is a consequence for such anger, and Your warnings make me aware so that I don't fall into the trap. I also know that my anger certainly does not honor You in any way. Your wisdom will be welcomed right now. I want my words to cause a peaceful calm to come over others like Yours did to the storm.

I crave to be a person who brings a healing phrase to hurting souls. Help me with Your words and wisdom so that I can accomplish the control I know You would want me to have. Make me a refreshment to others rather than a force for harm.

Your Apologetic Child

A LETTER FROM *Heaven*

Dear Apologetic Child,

I want you to take special note of what I am going to tell you: I want you to be eager to listen to others, slow to speak, and slow to become angry, because anger hinders the life I want you to have. A person with a short fuse stirs bad feelings, but a patient person brings calm to a quarrel. I want you to be like Me, for I am always full of grace, slow to become angry, and rich in love.

Do not allow anger to cause you to sin, and be sure to stop your anger before the end of the day. Otherwise, you will give the Evil One a chance to gain a hold on you. The wisdom that I give to you is above all pure, then peaceful, gentle, and easy to please. This wisdom is always ready to assist those who are in trouble and those who do good to others. It is always fair and honest.

You will find in your life that a gentle answer turns away wrath and that harsh words stir up anger. Be a kind and compassionate person to others, forgiving them with the same kind of forgiveness that I gave to you through Christ.

Your Understanding Father in Heaven

from James 1:19–20; Proverbs 15:18
Psalm 145:8; Ephesians 4:26–27; James 3:17
Proverbs 15:1; Ephesians 4:31–32

God's Word OF PROMISE

JAMES 1:19–20
My dear brothers, take note of this:
Everyone should be quick to listen,
slow to speak and slow to become
angry, for man's anger does not bring
about the righteous life that God
desires.

ECCLESIASTES 7:9
Do not be quickly provoked in your spirit,
for anger resides in the lap of fools.

PROVERBS 15:18
A hot-tempered man stirs up dissension,
but a patient man calms a quarrel.

PSALM 145:8
The LORD is gracious and
compassionate, slow to
anger and rich in love.

EPHESIANS 4:31–32
Get rid of all bitterness, rage and anger,
brawling and slander, along with every
form of malice. Be kind and compassionate to one another, forgiving each other,
just as in Christ God forgave you.

PROVERBS 15:1
A gentle answer turns away wrath,
but a harsh word stirs up anger.

JAMES 3:17
But the wisdom that comes from heaven is first of all pure;
then peace-loving, considerate, submissive, full of mercy
and good fruit, impartial and sincere.

EPHESIANS 4:26–27
"In your anger do not sin": Do
not let the sun go down while
you are still angry, and do not
give the devil a foothold.

A LETTER TO *Heaven*

Dearly Loved Father,

What I am writing to You about is extremely important to me. In fact, nothing could be more crucial to my future than this one thing. I have a great many things I want to accomplish in life, and I have carefully crafted the plans that will help me achieve my goals. However, I am also aware that nothing I can I dream, design, or devise will be accomplished or completed if You do not give it Your blessing. I am just one small person in a very large world, but You seem to take a special interest in fulfilling the magnificent with the mediocre and the sensational with the simple. You have anointed people who were considered insignificant and set them on thrones; You have selected the smallest of nations and made them mighty and powerful. You have even strengthened armies locked in battle that seemed all but lost and turned defeat into triumph.

I am asking for Your blessing on my hopes and dreams and also Your blessing on each step I take to accomplish what is set out before me. Bless me when I work and when I rest, when I run and when I walk, when I get discouraged and when I feel indestructible. With Your promise of blessing, I can begin my march toward tomorrow. I await Your words.

Your Blessed Child

A LETTER FROM *Heaven*

Dear Blessed Child,

You have made many plans and charted your course, but never forget that I am the one who will determine your steps. In everything you do acknowledge who I am, and I will make your paths straight. When I delight in where you are going, you can be sure that I will make your steps firm. I give countless blessings when you trust in Me. I will send a rainstorm of blessings.

Delight yourself in Me, and I will grant you the desires of your heart. Entrust your future hopes and dreams to Me, and this is what I will do: I will make your life shine like the dawn and your plans and purposes like the afternoon sun. This is My declaration to you: I know the plans I have for you, plans to prosper you and not to bring you harm, plans to confirm your hope and future. These blessings will fall on you and follow you if you obey Me. You will be blessed if you're in the city or in the country. You will be blessed when you are coming in and going out. I am with you and will save you; I will rejoice over you and you will rest in My love.

Your God of Blessing

from Proverbs 16:9; 3:6; Psalm 37:2
Romans 10:12; Ezekiel 34:26; Psalm 37:4–5
Jeremiah 29:11; Deuteronomy 28:2–3, 6

God's Word OF PROMISE

PROVERBS 3:6
In all your ways acknowledge him, and he will make your paths straight.

PROVERBS 16:9
In his heart a man plans his course, but the LORD determines his steps.

ROMANS 10:12
For there is no difference between Jew and Gentile—the same Lord is Lord of all and richly blesses all who call on him.

EZEKIEL 34:26
I will bless them and the places surrounding my hill. I will send down showers in season; there will be showers of blessing.

PSALM 37:23
If the LORD delights in a man's way, he makes his steps firm.

PSALM 37:4–5
Delight yourself in the LORD
and he will give you the desires
of your heart. Commit your
way to the LORD; trust in him
and he will do this.

DEUTERONOMY 28:2–3, 6
All these blessings will come upon you and
accompany you if you obey the LORD your
God: You will be blessed in the city and
blessed in the country. You will be blessed
when you come in and blessed when you
go out.

JEREMIAH 29:11
"For I know the plans I
have for you," declares
the LORD, "plans to
prosper you and not to
harm you, plans to
give you hope and a
future."

ZEPHANIAH 3:17
The LORD your God is with you, he is mighty to save. He
will take great delight in you, he will quiet you with his
love, he will rejoice over you with singing.

A LETTER TO *Heaven*

Dear God and Father,

Something is really bothering me, and I know that I will find the answers I need from You. Every day I wake up and all day long I seem to be nagged by an overwhelming sense of worry. It's not just one particular thing either. My mind jumps from one worry to another. One day I find myself concerned about money. Will I have enough to do the things I really want to do? Will I be able to save enough for when I retire? Will I have enough to help family and friends?

Then without warning I will begin worrying about my life. Will I live long? Will I catch a disease? Will I accomplish anything worth mentioning, or will I simply exist in the world and never really amount to much?

I read the paper and begin worrying about the state of the economy, the morality of our country, the thin peace that exists in the world, and the condition of the poor. I know that You do not want me to be consumed with such thoughts, but I am. I know that You do not worry about the present, past, or future. You have seen the beginning and end and know how all things will be and how all things will end. You hold tomorrow in Your hands and examine the seconds and the hours. What You see does not cause You to fear or fret. Help me to find assurance and confidence in Your power. Write soon and bring Your peace through Your promises.

Your Worried Child

A LETTER FROM *Heaven*

Dear Worried Child,

Just give all of your worries to Me, because I care deeply for you. Don't worry about anything, but in everything with a thankful heart, bring your prayers and requests to Me. My peace, which goes well beyond all human understanding, will protect your heart and mind in Christ. I will meet all your needs according to My own glorious wealth. I give authentic peace to those who depend on Me because they trust Me. Therefore, you can always trust Me because I am your rock forever.

I am telling you not to worry about your life, what you will eat or drink, or about your body, what you will wear. Isn't life more important than the food you eat or the clothes you wear? You will be like a tree with roots planted by the stream. It does not fear when heat comes, and its leaves are always green. It does not worry even in a drought, and it never fails to bear fruit.

Therefore, do not let tomorrow worry you; today has enough trouble of its own. You can be confident that in all matters I will work things out for your good because of your love and because you have been called to fulfill My purpose for you.

Your Assuring God

from 1 Peter 5:7; Philippians 4:6–7, 19; Isaiah 26:3–4
Matthew 6:25; Jeremiah 17:8; Matthew 6:34; Romans 8:28

God's Word OF PROMISE

PHILIPPIANS 4:6–7
Do not be anxious about anything, but in everything, by prayer and petition, with thanksgiving, present your requests to God. And the peace of God, which transcends all understanding, will guard your hearts and your minds in Christ Jesus.

ISAIAH 26:3–4
You will keep in perfect peace him whose mind is steadfast, because he trusts in you. Trust in the LORD forever, for the LORD, the LORD, is the Rock eternal.

PHILIPPIANS 4:19
And my God will meet all your needs according to his glorious riches in Christ Jesus.

1 PETER 5:7
Cast all your anxiety on him because he cares for you.

ROMANS 8:28
And we know that in all things God works for the good of those who love him, who have been called according to his purpose.

MATTHEW 6:25
Therefore I tell you, do not worry about your life, what you will eat or drink; or about your body, what you will wear. Is not life more important than food, and the body more important than clothes?

MATTHEW 6:34
Therefore do not worry about tomorrow, for tomorrow will worry about itself. Each day has enough trouble of its own.

JEREMIAH 17:8
He will be like a tree planted by the water that sends out its roots by the stream. It does not fear when heat comes; its leaves are always green. It has no worries in a year of drought and never fails to bear fruit.

A LETTER TO *Heaven*

Dear Father and Healer,

If it's true that trouble comes in waves, then I have been buried by a typhoon lately. I have been experiencing one of those odd times that defy understanding. Every move I make lands me in another hole, every turn I take runs me into another wall, and every decision I come up with turns out to be wrong. What a nightmare I have been living!

I turned to others for help and advice, but they either had their own troubles or could not give me any help with mine. They left me feeling even more desperate than before I approached them. I looked for answers from books, magazines, radio, and television. Every avenue I turned onto led me to a dead end. Then I turned to You.

What refreshment You brought me. Confidence replaced my concern. Hope appeared in my heart from nowhere. I don't know why I didn't run to You in the first place. You have always offered help in my troubles. Your torch of truth has been a constant source of light shining in the darkness. Thank You for carrying me on Your shoulders through the storm and shielding me from the wind and the rains that hammered against me. I raise my hands and heart in thanksgiving for Your help in my times of trouble. Thank You, thank You, thank You.

Your Trusting Child

A LETTER FROM *Heaven*

Dear Trusting Child,

Consider Me a safe place where you can hide, and I will protect you from trouble and surround you with my songs of deliverance. I am your shepherd who will not leave you in need. I will help you lie down in flourishing fields; I will show you quiet waters and refresh your soul.

Even if you find yourself walking through the dark valley of death, you will not fear any evil, because I am right there with you. You can rest assured that goodness and love will accompany you every day you live and that you will live in My house forever. I have told you these things so that you can find peace in Me. In this world you will have trouble, but here is My promise to you: I have overcome the world!

Your Protecting Father

from Psalms 32:7; 23:1–4, 6; John 16:33

God's Word OF PROMISE

PSALM 32:7
You are my hiding place;
you will protect me from
trouble and surround me
with songs of deliverance.

PSALM 91:10–11
Then no harm will befall you, no disaster
will come near your tent. For he will
command his angels concerning you to
guard you in all your ways.

JOHN 16:33
I have told you these
things, so that in me
you may have peace.
In this world you will
have trouble. But take
heart! I have overcome
the world.

PSALM 146:8
The LORD gives sight to
the blind, the LORD
lifts up those who are
bowed down, the LORD
loves the righteous.

PSALM 23:1–4, 6
The LORD is my shepherd, I shall not be in want. He makes me lie down in green pastures, he leads me beside quiet waters, he restores my soul. He guides me in paths of righteousness for his name's sake. Even though I walk through the valley of the shadow of death, I will fear no evil, for you are with me. Surely goodness and love will follow me all the days of my life, and I will dwell in the house of the LORD forever.

PSALM 73:26
My flesh and my heart may fail, but God is the strength of my heart and my portion forever.

NAHUM 1:7
The LORD is good, a refuge in times of trouble. He cares for those who trust in him.

PSALM 9:9
The LORD is a refuge for the oppressed, a stronghold in times of trouble.

A LETTER TO *Heaven*

Dear Father,

I couldn't believe I said it. In fact, when the words sprang from my mouth, it was as if I were hearing a stranger say them. It was in a conversation about current events. The talk wandered into the future, and before even realizing it, I made the awful statement: "Give me one reason to hope things will get better!" Where did those words come from? Did I really feel that hopelessness in my heart, or was it just a slip of the tongue, a momentary lapse? I am afraid to examine my heart for the answer.

I began to wonder if others saw that lack of faith in me. I've always wanted to be known for the hope that lived in me. I want to be a light of expectation that shines in the dark corners of this world and summons hope for others. This world needs the fragrance of hope, not the smell of despair.

Your words have always been like a refreshing breeze that tears away the gloom and restores desire and optimism. You have brought brightness back into eyes that were darkened by disease. You restore love into hearts that are infected by hatred. In You, the poor find riches and the weak find strength. Shower me with Your refreshing words of hope and restore what I have removed.

Your Child in Need of Hope

A *Letter from Heaven*

Dear Child in Need of Hope,

Why are you so sad in your spirit? Why so disturbed? If you'll put your hope in Me, you will have reason to be filled with praise. Be strong and encouraged, for I look out for those who respect Me and who hope in My unfailing love. I am a help and shield of protection for those who hope in Me.

My steadfast love and mercy never end. They are new every morning; great is My faithfulness. Say in your soul, "The Lord is mine so I hope in Him." I am always good to those who hope in Me and to those who search Me out. What will you say in response to all of this? If I am with you, who can ever defeat you? If I didn't even spare My own Son but gave Him up for you, is there anything I will keep from you? No, in everything you are more than a conqueror through My love.

Your God of Hope

from Psalms 42:11; 31:24; 33:18, 20
Lamentations 3:22–25; Romans 8:31–32, 37

God's Word OF PROMISE

PSALM 31:24

Be strong and take heart, all you who
hope in the LORD.

1 PETER 1:13

Therefore, prepare your minds
for action; be self-controlled; set
your hope fully on the grace to
be given you when Jesus Christ
is revealed.

PSALM 33:18, 20

But the eyes of the LORD are
on those who fear him, on
those whose hope is in his
unfailing love. We wait in
hope for the LORD; he is our
help and our shield.

PSALM 42:11

Why are you downcast, O my soul?
Why so disturbed within me? Put
your hope in God, for I will yet
praise him, my Savior and my God.

PSALM 71:5

For you have been my hope, O Sovereign LORD, my confidence since my youth.

LAMENTATIONS 3:22–25

Because of the LORD's great love we are not consumed, for his compassions never fail. They are new every morning; great is your faithfulness. I say to myself, "The LORD is my portion; therefore I will wait for him." The LORD is good to those whose hope is in him, to the one who seeks him.

ROMANS 8:31–32, 37

What, then, shall we say in response to this? If God is for us, who can be against us? He who did not spare his own Son, but gave him up for us all—how will he not also, along with him, graciously give us all things? In all these things we are more than conquerors through him who loved us.

PSALM 62:5–6

Find rest, O my soul, in God alone; my hope comes from him. He alone is my rock and my salvation; he is my fortress, I will not be shaken.

A LETTER TO *Heaven*

Dear Father,

You just can't imagine the things that I hear every day. Advertisements bombard me, promising that if I take a certain pill, purchase a particular piece of equipment, or watch a video, I will build the physique I've always dreamed of. Politicians promise that if cast my vote for the right person, I will pay less taxes, receive more services, and cure the problems of society. Day after day, more and more is promised and less and less is actually believable. It has begun to impact how I see, hear, and speak to everyone I come in contact with.

My soul hungers for authenticity. It hungers for real, relevant words that can be counted on as truth instead of the endless smoke screen of sentences that fog my world every day—truth that actually changes things from what they are to what I've always believed they could be.

Who can I believe? What is really right? And where do I find answers that will do more than empty my wallet and drain my trust? You are the one I turn to for truth. Through Your words I know I will find a reason to believe like a child again. Pour out Your promises on me and into my eager heart.

Your Child in Search of Truth

A LETTER FROM *Heaven*

Dear Searching Child,

My words are perfect, and they give new strength. The rules I have written can be trusted, and they make ordinary people wise. My decisions are true and completely right. My Word is a lamp to your feet that lights up the path you walk. My Word is alive and active. It is sharper than any double-edged sword; it penetrates even between the soul and spirit, the joints and bones. It evaluates what you think and the attitudes of your heart.

Love My teachings! Think about them all day long. My words are true from the start, and you will find that My rules for living are fair forever. You will be blessed when you read them and blessed when you let them soak into your heart. All Scripture is from My mouth and is useful for teaching, disciplining, correcting, and training, so that you are completely prepared to perform every good work. My Word is certain, and you will do well to pay attention to it, as if it were a light shining in a dark place until the day breaks and the morning star rises in your heart.

Your Father of Truth

from Psalms 19:7–9; 119:105; Hebrews 4:12
Psalm 119: 97, 160; Revelation 1:3
2 Timothy 3:16–17; 2 Peter 1:19

God's Word OF PROMISE

PSALM 119:97, 160

Oh, how I love your law! I meditate on it all day long. All your words are true; all your righteous laws are eternal.

2 PETER 1:19

And we have the word of the prophets made more certain, and you will do well to pay attention to it, as to a light shining in a dark place, until the day dawns and the morning star rises in your hearts.

PSALM 119:105

Your word is a lamp to my feet and a light for my path.

HEBREWS 4:12
For the word of God is living and active. Sharper than any double-edged sword, it penetrates even to dividing soul and spirit, joints and marrow; it judges the thoughts and attitudes of the heart.

REVELATION 1:3
Blessed is the one who reads the words of this prophecy, and blessed are those who hear it and take to heart what is written in it, because the time is near.

2 TIMOTHY 3:16–17
All Scripture is God-breathed and is useful for teaching, rebuking, correcting and training in righteousness, so that the man of God may be thoroughly equipped for every good work.

PSALM 19:7–9
The law of the LORD is perfect, reviving the soul. The statutes of the LORD are trustworthy, making wise the simple. The precepts of the LORD are right, giving joy to the heart. The commands of the LORD are radiant, giving light to the eyes. The fear of the LORD is pure, enduring forever. The ordinances of the LORD are sure and altogether righteous.

A LETTER TO *Heaven*

Dear God,

I just wanted to write and say thank You. You fill my life in so many ways that I am overflowing with gratitude. It is Your strength that I depend on and seek when I face obstacles and troubles, and it always comes in steady supply. Because it is Your power and not my own that is in me, I can live without fear. Triumphs have replaced the failures that had frequently forged their way into my daily life.

I am grateful also for the guidance You give. I follow where You lead, and I feel Your strong hand on my shoulder. Life is far less a mystery because You have shared with me the truth about my days on earth, the dangers that lie in wait for me, and where my help comes from. I find Your words, wisdom, and guidance faultless.

Even in the times that I fail You or weaken and worry, I know You are patient with me, wanting me to grow into the person only You can make me. You are my protection, power, hope, and strength. My soul will be filled with the gratitude You deserve. Thank You for revealing to me the life I could never have lived without You.

Your Thankful Child

A LETTER FROM *Heaven*

Dear Child,

My loved ones will always rest secure in Me, and those I love rest between My shoulders. Come to Me with thanksgiving and surround Me with praise; give thanks and honor to My name. My goodness and love goes on forever, and I will remain faithful to you through all time. I will strengthen you and bless you with peace. I am your light and your rescuer. Who can make you afraid? You are secure because I give you hope; you can look around you and rest safely. You can lie down without being afraid, and many will want to be your friend.

Even if the mountains are shaken and the hills disappear, My unfailing love for you will not be shaken, nor will My covenant of peace be taken away. I have great compassion for you. I am with you, and I am strong enough to save you. You give Me great pleasure. I will quiet you with My love and sing over you with great joy. I have come so that you can have the fullest life possible.

Your Loving God

from Deuteronomy 33:12; Psalms 100:3–4; 29:11; 27:11
Job 11:18–19; Isaiah 54:10; Zephaniah 3:17; John 10:10

God's Word OF PROMISE

PSALM 100:3–4

Know that the LORD is God. It is he
who made us, and we are his; we are
his people, the sheep of his pasture.
Enter his gates with thanksgiving
and his courts with praise; give
thanks to him and praise his name.

PSALM 27:11

Teach me your way, O LORD; lead me in a straight path
because of my oppressors.

DEUTERONOMY 33:12

Let the beloved of the
LORD rest secure in him,
for he shields him all day
long, and the one the
LORD loves rests between
his shoulders.

PSALM 29:11

The LORD gives strength to
his people; the LORD blesses
his people with peace.

JOB 11:18–19
You will be secure, because there is hope; you will look about you and take your rest in safety. You will lie down, with no one to make you afraid, and many will court your favor.

ZEPHANIAH 3:17
The LORD your God is with you, he is mighty to save. He will take great delight in you, he will quiet you with his love, he will rejoice over you with singing.

JOHN 10:10
I have come that they may have life, and have it to the full.

ISAIAH 54:10
"Though the mountains be shaken and the hills be removed, yet my unfailing love for you will not be shaken nor my covenant of peace be removed," says the LORD, who has compassion on you.

Other great gift books from Howard Publishing:

Heavenly Mail Series:
Heavenly Mail: Words of Encouragement from God

Hugs Series:
Hugs for Friends
Hugs for Dad
Hugs for Kids
Hugs for Mom
Hugs for Sisters
Hugs for Women
Hugs for Teachers
Hugs for Those in Love
Hugs for Grandparents
Hugs for the Holidays
Hugs for the Hurting
Hugs to Encourage and Inspire
Hugs for Grads
Hugs for Grandma

Hugs from Heaven Series:
Hugs from Heaven: Embraced by the Savior
Hugs from Heaven: On Angel Wings
Hugs from Heaven: The Christmas Story
Hugs from Heaven: Celebrating Friendship
Hugs from Heaven: Portraits of a Woman's Faith

Heartlifters Series:
Heartlifters for Mom
Heartlifters for Friends
Heartlifters for Women
Heartlifters for Hope and Joy
Heartlifters for Teachers
Heartlifters for the Young at Heart